M000278734

Looking For A Unicorn © 2019 by Kaya May

All rights reserved. Printed in the United States of America.
No part of this publication may for selling purposes be reproduced,
stored in a retrieval system, or transmitted without written permission
of the author. But if you want to post about the book online,
Post away babe. Post away.

www.kayamay.com

Photos & Design by Kaya May Media

Looking For A Unicorn

A BOOK OF POEMS, STORIES, & SECRETS

Table of Contents

The Beginning

CHAPTER ONE

Kaya May

I have spent all of my years
Looking for something
That may not exist.
Someone tall,
Strong,
Confident.
Gentle,
Funny,
Intelligent.
Motivated,
Humble,
Generous.
Athletic,
Talented,
Truly kind.
Wholesome,
Adventurous,
So hard to find.
I have been looking
Since the day I was born.
I am looking for a unicorn.

I looked for it in every room tonight
For the chance that someone might
Catch my eye and catch my name
Play his cards and play the game
Grab my hand, spin me around
In a Nashville bar downtown

You have long blonde hair and a starting spot
On the football team
You are so entirely
Out of my league
You're popular and tall and
Play guitar on the side
If I'm only yours when you're bored
That is completely fine

I've said it without saying it 100,000 times
I DON'T WANT TO BE JUST FRIENDS
I'm screaming from inside
Tell me how to be more clear
I'm screaming and
You cannot hear

You make it hard not to be easy.

My name sounded so pretty
Coming from your mouth
I don't think I've wanted anyone
More than I do now

I said I'm glad you came to class
And that made you laugh
I haven't stopped hearing that
For five entire days
I try to think of other things
And all I see's your face

You're majoring in accounting
But you should minor in me
Since you're so good with numbers
Mine's one you should keep

Kaya May

Some people want to change the world
I just want to be a part of yours

My heart actually stopped beating
When your name showed up on my screen
I thought I fell for another boy
Who couldn't care less about me

I know it's not fair to put that kind of pressure on you
To be the reason I am finally happy
But then what do people mean
When they say "you complete me"
Doesn't that imply
That you weren't completely whole before
If there's something missing
What's so wrong with wanting more
Why do I have to love myself
Before someone else can love me too
I'd love me so much more
If I were loved by you

Next time you're next to me
Don't leave your hands in your lap
Next time our faces get that close
Let's just close the gap

This could be the start of something
Far better than what I've had
I've only ever wanted
What didn't want me back
I've been waiting and praying
For someone like you
For a dozen years
I think today I can say
That he's finally here

I Met You Yesterday

Seeing you walk down the street- me telling my friend that wow you
were cute and getting out of the car to sit next to you - me asking which
part of town you were headed to hoping it was the same as mine -
will be one of the better memories of my little life

You coming into the same train car as me and asking to sit in my seat -
talking about our favorite bands and our families - how yours sounded
like it was a lot like mine -
will be one of the better memories of my little life

Hearing the conductor say we were nearing our stop, watching you
scramble for your phone and asking if it would be okay to keep in touch
- knowing I'd never wanted anything that much - with seventy five
strangers filing out of the station in line
will be one of the better memories of my little life

Stumbling off the sidewalk after we got lunch in the middle of the next
afternoon because neither of us can ever be on time - you pulling me
back and putting your hand in mine
will be one of the better memories of my little life

Kaya May

I Met You Yesterday

Leaving you with people I barely knew and coming back to you making
everyone smile as if they were just as much your friends as they were mine
will be one of the better memories of my little life

Hearing you tell me you'd been taking the train for two whole years and no
one new had ever talked to you - that how it happened was just like you'd
seen it in your mind
will be one of the better memories of my little life

Watching you stand at the top of the stairs of my best friend's apartment
saying you didn't want to go to work hoping that you'd want to make this
work - after spending sixteen hours straight with me- you saying
"Maybe I can see you tonight?"
will be one of the better memories of my little life

Looking For A Unicorn

It's so easy for me to fall in love
With someone who has a sweet soul
All you have to be for me
Is internally beautiful

22

We were two kids kissing in a parking lot
Because that's what people do
I think I'll write your name on my heart
Because it belongs to you

I told you infinity isn't long enough
And I made a joke about it
But I'd need forever to get used to this
I don't know how I lived so long without it

They looked at me like I was crazy. Out of my mind for wanting you-
for even entertaining the idea. We were too young, they said. But I
don't know, I guess I just don't believe that love knows what numbers
are, or really cares about them. I don't care about them. I could be 80
years old meeting you for the first time and I'd still love you. By then
no one would care about the amount of years between us. I want all
of the rest of my years between us. I don't care what people say. They
can look all they want with that surprise on their face- but my love I
will love you the same.

The Middle

CHAPTER TWO

Kaya May

How do I discover your favorite color
And the reasons you're not with her
How do I go from dinner with you on a Tuesday
To the face in the frame on your desk at work
How do I get a spare key to your apartment
So I can come by when I want
How do I convince you to
Decide I'm what you want
Because I'm not sure how to be in love
I've never done this before
The girl I was when I was loved
Is not me anymore

I sat here thinking I was going to wait for someone
Who wanted to know who I was when I was seventeen
And then I realized you already knew
Everything about me
You were the only thing that stayed
When I always had to leave
So why would I settle for someone
That I have to teach
Who may not even want to know
The reasons I am who I am now
I don't have to explain to you
You already know how
I grew up in a little town and moved around a lot
And I'd never found a boy I liked enough to settle down
About my brother and my parents and our family's first dog
My best friends and the loose ends of the things that I forgot
You were there when I was still deciding who I wanted to be
I've wanted you to be with me
Since I was seventeen

As you went to kiss me
You said "You're dangerous"
And I just nodded my head
I know when you play with fire
You end up vibrant or dead

I see love in your eyes and that scares me to death
Because I know I don't love you yet
Sometimes I want to say it because I love who you are
But there's a difference between a love from the head
And a love from the heart

I wish I could want you
The way that you want me
But when someone says they'll stay
All I want to do is leave
You made this too easy
You made this too hard
Kissing my forehead, cheeks and nose
In the front seat of my car
Handing me the pieces
Of your unrequited heart

I think maybe I could love you someday,
But I don't love you right now
All my life I've tried to reciprocate
But I haven't learned how
I love the way you untie my shoes when I'm tired from dancing
The way you said making me smile is your new favorite thing
How you brought me cheesecake on Valentine's Day and a stuffed
Animal to commemorate my best friend that passed away
How you said you wished you had more hands so you could hold
More of me
How you always say that you don't ever want to leave
How you show up late and that's good for me because I'm
Never ready on time
How I said I wasn't ready for a relationship and you said that was fine
But I get this pit in my stomach when I think about how
I don't feel the way that you do now
I still want to meet new people and dance
With strangers on Saturdays
And I don't know if it's you or if it's a phase
Because I can't tell if I'm too young and not ready to be tied down
Or if I just don't love the boy
Who gave my head a crown

"But can you miss someone you've never met?"

"Yes," I said,

"I do it every day."

I swear he looks at me
And you're still all I see
If you two stood side by side
I'd choose you every time
So,
What happens when we're all grown up
And marrying other people
What happens when we're settled down in separate towns-
Saying "I do"
And I'm
Still
In love with you

"How are you two?"
"We're just fine"
"Is she the one?"
"She's a nice girl"

"You should be with"

Delete
Delete
Delete

"I'm happy
You're happy"

I came across the first picture I ever took of you
Across the table in a t-shirt
That smile that when you wanted something,
It would always work

You were so innocent
You hadn't done so many things yet
And I wanted to be your first
But you just wanted to hook up
I'd give anything for you

To un-give it up

Kaya May

You said you missed me all the time
That if I just came to you then we'd be fine
Said we could move out wherever I liked
As soon as you got done with school
I know you didn't mean it
But the idea of it was cool

.

How strange it is that he tries so hard
And you don't try at all
And I know that he would answer
But you're the one I call

Kaya May

You're the dead end road that I
Always find myself on
The thing I keep trying to make right
That will always be wrong

I know he doesn't mean it but at least he says he's sorry.

You're leaving for the summer
So I don't see the point
You'll find somebody better
And leave me with no choice
I'll be missing you in May and June
Comparing someone else to you
In the middle of July
In August I'll make up an excuse
And then tell him goodbye

Looking For A Unicorn

I'd like to hang up a map and take a tack
To the places you loved other girls
Then I know I'd finally be
Your entire world

I called you out about her
And you said you didn't know what I meant
You tucked your tail and bit your tongue and said
She's just a friend

This cotton candy sky-
That's what you are like
With words that mean nothing to me
For they are as insubstantial
As they are sweet

Kaya May

Don't tell me I'll be fine after
Because I was fine before
I'm not interested
In just fine anymore

I woke myself up because you aren't the one
That I'm supposed to be dreaming of
This new boy he wants me, treats me so good
Says all the things that I know he should
He's even almost as good of a man as you are
He's taking my time but you took my heart
Cause maybe I miss your little sister
And how before bed you'd lean down and kiss her
Maybe I miss your house and your hands
Watching old home movies of you and your friends
All I remember are all the good things
And I'm the girl who looked at you
And said "I have to leave"

Kaya May

I was on my way out of town
I didn't think anything could make
Me want to turn around
But I swear I saw you in my rearview
And in my speakers coming through

Saying, "Lady, you don't have to leave
I think you could be what's good for me
What's the rush anyway
The rest of the world can wait
Just come back to me and stay"

But I was getting on to getting gone
With a suitcase and a tank of gas
I packed up all the memories
Didn't leave a string attached

"But you've got time to see it all
The rest of time to fly and fall
For every coast and pretty city
But if you leave it won't be with me
Lady just come back and stay
The rest of the world can wait"

I fell for you so hard I
Think I actually broke on impact with the ground
I never liked boys with brown eyes and
They're all that I like now
Forget everyone else who tries to talk to me
The next four months apart
Pennsylvania and a boy in it
Took my whole Midwest heart

I have a screenshot of a text you sent me after I asked
If you were seeing the girl in your pictures
If you were happy with her

"I wasn't 'seeing' her, but we were going on dates on some
weekends. I wasn't the wanting to stay up with her til 2,
walking Chicago, playing cornhole, losing casino type of
happy the way I was with you."

I told you maybe you were the one
With a future in poetry
I still wish you were the one
With a future with me

You are nothing that I was looking for
I was so much more
Vibrant before

How do you remember
The way that you once felt
How do you stop the snow
Before it all just melts

How do you stop the rain
When it's already in the clouds
How do you convince a boy
To love who you are now

You said you wanted to dive into me
But don't you remember what they say
When the water's too deep?
"Swim at your own risk, no life guard on call"
Not responsible if you slip and fall
I wasn't trained to save someone who's sinking
I never said I could save you from thinking
That I was the one or I was it for you
I never said I'd rescue you
I had caution written across my face
Don't act like you didn't see it and stay

Your voice sounds a lot like his
And I'm surprised that I miss
Anything about you after all this time

I ended things, you got married,
And I should be fine

Not sitting here hearing your voice
On the other end of the line

I want someone with the looks of you
And the heart of him
I want the halves of two whole people and
I
Can't
Win.

There's a patch of skin on my chin
That's scratched rough from your scruff
It's been four days- it won't go away
And I've had enough
Of waking up reminded of you
By the stupid mirror
You shouldn't have a hold of me
When you're not even here

You said my poems have been rather angry lately
And I laughed to myself
Wait till you read the things I'll write
About you once you've left

The Other

CHAPTER THREE

I'm looking for it elsewhere
Cause you don't give me what I need
Just because you said it once
Doesn't mean I still believe
Why do you think I keep
Posting pictures of myself
If you won't call me beautiful
I'll find it somewhere else

My love don't lose yourself
In the fear of losing him

Forever stands in front of you- holding out her hands
But yours are both closed in fists- you don't understand
That to keep someone like her
You must first be a man

You don't have social media
And I guess that's good for me
Now you'll never know how many poems I wrote
For boys that chose to leave

You see, it doesn't flatter me
When you call me pretty
I want to hear about my soul
How that's what makes me beautiful
I want you to see that I'm smart
And not like all of the girls you've known
But all you seem to like about me
Is what your eyes are shown
What about if we were blind
Would you still want me then?
I don't want to be beautiful
I want to be magnificent

It actually bothers me
When you 'like' my stuff online
Because I'd much rather you just
Liked me in real life

Kaya May

This stupid airport
I've been here so many times
Too many strangers
Have seen me cry
And I love you but not enough
To forfeit my dreams
I chose you every time
But this time I choose me

God knew how special he made you and how much
I'd love you so he made you my brother so that you'd be
The first boy I loved that didn't leave

I wish I didn't want to be
More like you and less like me
I wish I was pretty when I woke up
I wish I was someone that someone loved
I wish I didn't wish so much
I wish I could just live
Instead of living up

In the backseat of my parents' Nissan rental car I came up with my favorite person in the world's wedding hashtag and simultaneously felt my heart break inside my chest. But this time it was a different sort of breaking. When boys had hurt me- every couple months or so for the entirety of my life- those kinds of hurts compared more to fractures- something that always mended one way or another- but this time it is permanent.

My brother is getting married. All I can think about is sitting next to him when we were both still in college watching a stupid cartoon movie that I begged him to see, eating peanut butter toast laughing until we cried- the happiest I'd ever been. My best friend. I've never felt better about myself than I did with him. And it will never be just us again.

From this day on one of his hands and half of his mind will be preoccupied. And maybe it would hurt less, if I had someone, but I've never had someone. I am not sure how to function in a world where everyone I have ever loved found something or someone that they loved more than they loved me.

My sweet Momma says I'm brave but is it brave to sit on
your carpet crying till you can barely breathe and not know
if anything in the world could get you to get up out of that
room unless it was her walking back into it?

I'm learning to be more gentle.
With those toilet paper sheets in airports because if you
pull them with too much force they'll just tear and be
useless. With my mother when I used to snap at her
because I knew she would still love me if I did. And
with myself too. More gentle to the girl I've spent so
many years saying she's not smart enough, fun enough,
interesting enough, pretty enough for someone to love.
I will learn to become content with the body and brain I
have while I'm here. I'll learn to be more gentle
with the girl in the mirror.

Kaya May

You think you're not good enough for them. Oh but you are. Those big vibrant eyes- pretty lips, pretty hair, pretty, pretty heart. So much more to offer as you are versus what you aren't. It isn't about being attractive or worthy enough. You have always been enough. Do you know what it really is? It is that the majority of our generation is not ready to settle down. They see you and they think- they're one I'd end up with- but you know what- they aren't ready to end up with anyone. This is the most frustrating, confusing thing in the world for you right now. I get it. I've never convinced someone to like me back for more than a couple weeks. I haven't been in a relationship since my senior year of high school. I'm 23. I have full faith that there will be someone who comes along and makes you feel a resounding sigh of relief- "wow, this is why it never worked before." I'm not even worried about you. All you can do in the waiting is become more like the kind of person you'd like to marry. Do you want them to be trustworthy? You can use this time to become better at keeping your word. Do you want them to be a good conversational- ist? You can use this time to be intentional about what you talk about with your friends and family and acquaintances and strangers- you can cultivate yourself into the version of you that you're most proud of. This way every day waiting is not wasted- you are improving and growing and when they find you, you will be more ready for yourself and for them. I know the waiting is hard. I've been doing it my whole life. But I am here to tell you that you are indeed worthy of whatever it is you seek. And that it will come in perfect timing.

Pretty is stupid. I want to be loved.

Smart.

Helpful.

Funny.

Pretty will fade and be forgotten.

How you made them feel will not.

You said you "liked" my music.

My music I put five straight years and 5,000 hours

And my whole heart into

You "liked it"

Wow

What a compliment

Do you realize what you've just said?

You've lumped me into ranch dressing

And the paint color on your walls

And the stupid songs your meatheaded friends

Listen to on the squat rack

You like those things

Just as much,

Probably more

Than you "liked" my music

You may as well have slapped me across both my cheeks

That would be the equivalent of what you've just said to me

People, places, things, and melodies can be toxic to your well-being. That person who when you make something you have spent whole days working on- what you have embedded your actual spirit into- when they look at it and nod and say it "looks good" and in that moment you feel the dictionary definition of empty- you do not need to feel that way. You must not feel that way as much as it is up to you. Do not bring your treasures to those who see them as trash. It is like they wear sunglasses and cannot see your light. You are shining whether or not they can see. I am learning that your childhood dreams don't have to come to fruition, and you don't have to be sad when they don't- or if they do for someone else. No, haven't you grown? Haven't you changed? Why should you be expected to become a star just because that's what you wanted when you were still making dolls have conversations and letting your mother choose what you wore to school? No babe, you are allowed to change. You can realize maybe you'd like to make a career out of something else after you've already spent five years in school studying something you'd really rather die than do for the rest of your life. You can cut all of your hair off or dye it purple because you want to. You can start a business. You can babysit other people's kids as a full-grown adult when all your friends seem to be married and having their own because you know what - they're spending money taking care of them and you're making it. You can do what you want with today, and tomorrow, and your whole full-of-possibilities life. I believe in you. Even if you don't.

Kaya May

It was pouring rain in my car when you told me you hated yourself
I wish you could see the way that you are seen
By everyone else

I think as women we feel it but don't say it
And they say it
But don't feel it

I love my mother, she
Is helpful, gentle, and kind
But the manual for how she works
Is not the same as mine
For every way she is soft she is equally as strong
If what she's getting isn't right she will work till it's not wrong
My whole life my mother tried to make me into
The kind of girl who wore a purse, used her inside voice
Did what the good girls do
But I am the kind who is told to quiet down in class
"Don't be so loud in front of boys-
Hold back when you laugh"
My whole life my mother tried to fluff my hair up for more volume
While in every other way she tried to turn me down
"Maybe be a little less, a little less loud"
My whole life my mother tried
To make me stay in a town
Where people stay in their lanes,
Decorate and settle down
Where dreams stay dreams and safe stays safe
And kids just stay kids
My whole life my mother tried
To make me who she is

You see, almost anything tastes good when you're starving.
This statement can unfortunately be applied to relationships. When
you feel as if no one's wanted you for a long time- when you're
so entirely hungry for love and someone, when anyone gives you
a taste of it- it's going to taste so much better than it would if you
hadn't already been so hungry. We need to be more cognizant of our
emotions and how they skew our perceptions of love and other
people. If you've had the worst day- you're annoyed and angry-
meeting with someone then would have an entirely different out-
come than if you'd met with that same person when you felt good
about your life. Please do not confuse your feelings with reality,
or worse confuse them as being the same.

You said "I just wanted you to know
That I'm not with her anymore
She thinks there's something in her future
That wasn't there before"
And I shook my head and said
You may no longer be what you once were
But your heart
Is still with her

She's like me but prettier
But I cant help but pity her
For having to do all the things I would not
Let you keep going when you should stop
She mustn't have many thoughts of her own
For there's no room for two
On the seat of your throne
And does she make you laugh ever or at all
Or just sit at the foot of your soapbox
And pick up when you call

You were so incredibly flattering
Your words were so convincing
But you only want it till it's yours
I guess you only knock
On closed doors

Sometimes you just have to let it go
You realize that thing will never stop hurting you
No matter how much time goes by
That the only way you can stop feeling that way
Is if you get rid of the reminders
Unfollow them
Delete the picture
Stop checking in
Sometimes time doesn't heal the wound
But you can choose to stop taking off the bandages

You sat next to me on a plane
For one whole hour
You know we could've learned so much
If it'd run out of power
Funny how you choose a device
That doesn't know you
Over someone who's sitting here
Saying she wants to
I'd compliment your hair and eyes
And your sweet, gentle smile
But you'd rather play with your phone
Like a little child

Birthday Cake Jones Soda
Tastes like summertime
I find the sugar on my lips
Tastes like you're still mine

My mom calls the boys that are hard to let go of, but not exactly
what we need "Mr. Almost Right." I've met a lot of them. I really
don't think you need to be discouraged because every time you meet
one you're a step closer to Mr. Actually Right. I know that sounds
silly but I know it's also true. You're too good to settle for someone
who doesn't really love you. You are too exceptional in too many ways
to be with someone you're not very excited about or worse-
who doesn't treat you very well. I know you'll find him.
I hope you find him soon.

I think life's two hardest things are forgiving someone who isn't sorry
And forgetting someone you didn't want to leave

Basically don't take anything anyone says verbatim. If someone tells you something bad about someone you don't know- don't believe a word of it. People describe people through a foggy lens of negative emotions. They talk down on others because they either made them feel excluded, they wish they were closer to them, or their confidence bothers them because they are insecure. There is never a reason to believe any negative thing about anyone unless you drew the conclusion on your own from an in-person experience. Even then, can't we be gracious? People are mean. Please don't be like them.

This is what I've looked at
Every day for the past year and a half
Bright colors on a computer screen
That track the words that I sing
A friend with more talent than almost anyone I know
Sunshine coming in strong through the same window

Sometimes I wish I could stay
Do two more years and graduate
I want to make everyone happy
To not make my mom cry when I talk about leaving
To be close to my brother and go to his games
To keep at least some of the friends that I've made
I never wanted to have to make life-changing choices
I'm afraid
I'll miss their voices

But I've been trying to make everyone happy
For almost all my years
And I'm
Not happy here

Kaya May

You are just
One red light
On my happy street
And I know I won't lose hope
For the light will soon turn green

Settling

I think some of the most important advice I could give someone is to stop settling for things that hurt.

I am not saying that if something in general is challenging that you should forfeit it, but I am saying you may consider considering it when it comes to this. If you're waiting by the phone hoping they will contact you- a snap, a text, a like.. if waiting hurts and not knowing makes you feel like you're quite frankly dying inside- baby love, this is not it for you. It doesn't have to be extravagant, but I'm also telling you it doesn't have to be confusing, stressful, or saddening.

A romantic relationship is meant to be fun. It is an add on- an accessory- it is not essential for anything. You can live and breathe and grow and thrive as a completely solo entity. I've been single for almost the entirety of my life. I can count the amount of boyfriends I've had on half a hand and I have never loved someone who loved me. But there is Someone who has always loved me. The love of Jesus Himself is fully satisfactory- leaving no necessity for any additional love, BUT because He loves us so much He gives us the opportunity to love and be loved by others. He will bring you some- one. Be patient. And would you PRAY about it. He knows the desires of your heart, and I do not doubt that He will fulfill them- but I also do not doubt that He may be testing you in this time before you meet them. I feel like God repeatedly asks me, "Do you love Me most?"

Kaya May

Settling

He wants to be the most important thing in our life. He does not desire this selfishly, but for our own good. He knows that once He is our priority, everything else is more successful at a less-elevated level. Once you value God and His commandments over everything else, He tends to bring you favor in everything else.

What I ultimately am trying to say is- be you absolutely fully- just try to stop TRYING so hard. The person you marry will eventually discover all the things you've been hiding in your calculated process of capturing and keeping them. If they don't stay, you know they weren't the one for you. You are completely okay as just you. Not you once you lose the weight or lose the bad skin- and not you once you get more followers or lash extensions. Not you minus something, not you plus something. Stop being so hard on yourself. What an exhausting life it would be feeling like you had to impress someone for the rest of forever in order to keep them around.

I know it sounds too simple. You're thinking "no one is going to just drop someone in front of me without me doing anything," but I'm here to tell you that your chances of finding love actually become greater as your involvement in the pursuit of it becomes lesser. Refuse to settle for what is not best for you, and what is best will be there soon.

You were the closest thing I'd ever seen
To something being right for me
But I don't think that I've been
On the same clock as God
I think it might be time that I
Got a different watch

I'm learning that it's okay not to agree with the person next to you,
or even your best friend or your parents. That it's okay to not want to
get out of your sweatshirt on a Friday night. That anyone who stops
caring for you as a result of what you look like never really cared
about you at all. I'm learning that every day is an opportunity to show
the love of Jesus. The airport, the restaurant, the Uber. I'm learning
I never regretted making someone's life better, even if it was at my
own expense. I've learned to stop eating once you're full. I've learned
that some girls will be able to eat whatever they want whenever they
want and not gain a pound- and that there are equally as many girls out
there "worse" off than you- and that NONE. OF. THAT. MATTERS.
You're a size 2? Cool, so was I in 3rd grade. I guarantee your beauty is
not equivalent to the number on your tag. And if someone makes you
feel like it is, you need to hang around different someones. Jeez. Stop
spending all your time with people that model for a living. Life makes
you feel bad enough- there's no reason to further subject yourself to
insecurity. And the most important thing: everyone I love on earth will
hurt me, but not the one in Heaven. All He has ever done is love, and
that is all He will ever do. He has never and will never stop loving you.

I've been there. It was bad. I've spent many hours of my life covering up and editing out the spots on my face. I hated myself. But I did learn through that process how to find confidence within (because I didn't have it in my appearance) and also that people just don't notice or care about the things we worry so much about. When I see "issues" on someone's face I don't think one single negative thing about it. I think, oh, that's a pimple, that's a scar, I have those, and I don't notice again. It is so much more important to treat someone with respect and care - and if you do that - if they are still bothered by your or some-one else's appearance- then they are no longer worth spending another second of time thinking about or standing beside.

Kaya May

The expectation is perfection and doesn't look a thing like me
I will never meet the standard of the magazine
My eyes will never be that saturated, my waist will never be that small
The only thing that we share is that we're both too tall
I can't shrink my ribcage or make my cheekbones more intense
I can't be your trophy wife
Within your picket fence

It's not necessarily
That I needed to be pretty
I just wanted you to think I was

Kaya May

She had scattered thoughts,
Scattered shoes,
Messy hair,
And a messy room

But she could make you clean

There are pictures of smiling people all over my walls
How can it be that we no longer speak at all
But I can't place blame or say it's either of our faults
Because we both sat back and watched
As we sputtered and then stalled

But I could've saved that love and saved that time
Saved my heart and saved my mind
If you always knew that you would leave
Why did you even come
I wish when I had the chance
That I would've run

Kaya May

Living in Nashville is kind of like
Falling in love with someone who doesn't know your name
I think the possibility of being known someday
Is what makes us choose to stay

You're like a red zinfandel
You get sweeter with age
I wish you were with me
Laughing on this plane

Kaya May

Yesterday a man told me I was pretty, two strangers did tonight
But every time these words come to me they translate through as lies
I have my own room and more clothes than I need and I am writing
This on a computer I didn't pay for on my own
But I want a boyfriend and a best friend that doesn't live five hundred
Miles away and I want someone to take care of me like they did when I
Was young - I want someone to care that I don't have someone
I want tan skin and long hair and perfect, perfect teeth
I want perfect pitch and a job I like and for someone to think of me
As something more than pretty
I want more hours to write and play guitar and take pictures of my friends
But I wake up go school go to work and do it over and over again
I don't think that I can keep doing this on my own
But I've almost hit twenty-three and I am still alone
I know I'm privileged and ungrateful
And that only makes me more sad
For I cannot get over
The things that I can't have

I've been posing for pictures for 23 years
And still don't know what to do with my hands
I've been trying to date since the seventh grade
And still don't know how to keep a man
I told my father I'd marry a nice boy
That loved Jesus like I did
But I didn't know he'd be so hard to find
Or if he even exists
Because half the boys I meet these days
Only want to kiss my face
And the other half don't even
Want a second date
It seems the ones that I want
Never feel the same
I've tried hair up, hair down,
Snapchat filter flower crown
Big smile, look away,
I've tried the leave, I've tried the stay
I've tried to be more like me, less like me,
And nothing ever works
I think the only way he'll want me
Is if I'm just like her

Kaya May

I found myself in tears at church
And no one seemed to care
Often times I wonder if
I was even there

One girl stands off alone
I wonder why she strayed
I wonder if she left
Because no one said to stay

Kaya May

You have a broken umbrella
And a broken heart
I wish you knew
How lovely you are

This morning I unzipped my suitcase
And sand flew out at me
I would give anything
To have it back beneath my feet
I went to pull up my hair
And found sand between my fingers
I find that I find pieces of myself
In the scent of sea that lingers

I love the hair on my legs
It is indicative of the time I've been
Waiting for him
It tells of the night after night I spent sleeping alone,
Waiting for him
It is a reason I can't settle for someone like you-
I am sorry- I'm
Waiting for him

I am a woman
I have hair on my limbs
And when I find the one I want to share my life with
I will shave away all of the days I spent
Waiting
For him

The End

CHAPTER FOUR

Potholes
Burrito bowls
Mountains and strawberritas
The airport
Colorado
And after church lunch pizza
The Office, Wal-Mart,
Home-made scrambled eggs
My chapped lips, wideset hips,
The bruises on my legs
George Strait, my pink suitcase
And springtime flag football
All these things attached to you
And we're not attached at all

Someone asked me about you and my trip to Colorado

And I wondered how I was to explain 1 month and 84 straight

Hours of falling in love in the two minutes of their attention span

I started to say that it was complicated, stopped and told her the truth

That you are perfect, it was perfect, and I'm not good enough for you

Kaya May

Baggage Claim

That's the thing about meeting someone on Saturday night
They don't tell you when they drink they smoke cigarettes
And when they're drunk that they fight
That their parents split five years ago and there's a wound
Where Dad should've loved them better
That they swear too much and don't believe in God and their
Plans change like the weather
That they live two and a half hours away and in the morning
They will go away
No my minutes with you in a bar downtown
Didn't begin to tell me about
Your skeletons, your suitcases, your significant flaws
The truth under the shiny facade
For the dirt and dust can't be noticed at all
Beneath the buzz of alcohol

His love language is touch
And conveniently it's mine
But we were only good
At talking between the lines

Stupid Cupid

You picked me up like I weighed five pounds
Took my hands in the kitchen and spun me around
Let me stand on your feet and walked while I laughed
Sat me on your couch and told me that
You hadn't been happier in quite a long time
That your favorite face would have to be mine
That there was a scale
Of 1 to me
That I had a pretty
Personality
That I had the best lips
That you'd ever kissed
And I thought I shot my arrows
But I must've missed

Silly girl, Superman
Wasn't made to stay
All he knows is to go
Trained to fly away

Kaya May

My mind is a galaxy
You don't care to explore
My body is a map
You travel when you're bored
My heart is an ocean
You didn't want to swim
My future is a record
You didn't want to spin
My love is a river
That would never run dry
And your heart is a bridge
That doesn't lead to mine

I wish I could fully feel the significance of a moment. I wish I could grasp the magnitude of my wishes being granted and not just the reality of them not living up to what I wanted. You were someone's boyfriend that I wished I had- clicking through your pictures thinking you were who should be with me but you already had someone that made you happy and the next thing I know you've broken up and I'm in your house at a party and your hand is on my shoulder saying it's good to finally meet me and one week later you're in my room saying "don't you want to kiss me" and your leather jacket's on my floor and I'm asking you to leave.

Kaya May

I told you that we couldn't be
What we were anymore
I changed my mind and you changed
What you were looking for

We thought it was love but it was just a moment
It's not wrong that we took it and we owned it
We held hands and posted pictures and kissed on the street
It's okay to realize you love someone and someone isn't me
We didn't know better, or know what we were
I was what you loved before love became her

Kaya May

The last thing you ever said to me was "Goodbye pretty girl"
And I said under my breath "You're not allowed to call me that"
You can't call me the name you'll call
The next girl you love back
For you only led me on just like they always do
And I just can't believe
This time it was with you

The worst part about it is
I only think good things of you
There is not a single flaw
In any thing you do
Even the way you let me go
Was honest gentle and kind
You are everything I need you to be
Everything but mine

I'm in the same damn town as you and I can't even see you
Because you started seeing someone else

If you wonder if I'm over you
The answer is still no
It's been six months and I
Just wanted you to know

Kaya May

It was 11:28am when I thought I heard your laugh
I didn't know my heart had mended
Till I felt it break in half

I hope a blonde steals your heart
And your time and your money
I hope she tells you the truth-
That you're not actually funny
I hope you have too much to drink
And the best night of your life
Wake up and can't remember
A minute of your time

Kaya May

I don't miss you but I miss your arms around me
And I wonder if that's the same thing

I put my hands on your body
Just to remind you I'm in the room
But you couldn't care less
What I do
So I don't know why you
Went out of your way
To have me here
I'm just taking up

Space

In your atmosphere

Kaya May

I could fill an ocean with promises that didn't come true
With things you said only because you knew
You were acquiring gold stars in my book
Finessing a heart you already took
You are set in your ways and though you tried
You will never love anyone like
The way you pamper and dote on yourself
For there isn't enough love in your heart for anyone else

It's as if all the wind in the world
Got behind your boat
The second I got on board
Your ship sailed but I was still there
And you didn't even know

Kaya May

I sat in the back of my father's car
And cut off my split-ends with kitchen scissors
Kind of like you cut me off
And got together with her

How did you manage to say
So many things right
Hang my heart among the stars
You had me so high
You made me feel so confident
And then took that away
As if your ability to control me
Made me want to stay

Kaya May

Sometimes when I
Come across your things
I absentmindedly start to think
I'm still in the time where you still love me

You built me up like an English tower
But instead of rock
Your bricks were made of flour
So all my walls came crumbling down
And all you see is ugly now
I know now this is why I shouldn't open up
Every time I do someone falls out of love

Kaya May

I have a note in my phone with 23 names of boys I kissed
I don't even remember number 22 on that list
I looked at the parentheses: "Foreign guy downtown Chi"
And found myself saying aloud- "Was I really that drunk?"
I must've missed you so much
I'd erase numbers 1 through 20 and 22 to 23
If I could have you back to me
You were the 21st and I was 21
And you are the only boy I ever loved
Who said he loved me back
I never thought I'd ever get
To ever feel like that
But every odd was stacked against us
And we tried so hard to out-run time
But it was faster than us
You cut off all your hair and you came up on my phone
I didn't recognize you at first and you weren't alone
"She's beautiful" you captioned it
With a girl who's nothing like what you said you wanted
And for the first time I hate you for coming into my life
For I may have never known how it felt to be loved
If you hadn't come by

Looking For A Unicorn

Screw you, I just miss your dog

It's funny how someone I spent
One month short of one year on
Could go from me so painlessly
From good to great to gone
You posted a picture of a girl I knew
And you haven't realized it yet
But maybe I was just a stepping stone
To someone you hadn't met

I'm never going to see your face again or hold it in my hands
I'll never see you graduate or become a good man
I'll never watch your eyes light up unless it's in a video
And to this day I don't know why
I ever let you go

I just wanted to love you forever, that's all

I never said "I love you"
But I wrote it in my songs.
So I'll stand before a hundred souls
And let them sing along

February 2nd, 2016
The day that you stopped wanting me
Said that you had found somebody else
And it wasn't me
Said God already had someone picked out
I thought that you were him until now
And I guess sometimes that's the way it works
He picked you for her

She better have the brightest eyes you've ever seen
Like she could've walked out of a magazine
She better have a pretty name and tiny waist
A heart that's as just pretty as her stupid face
She better break records for how smart she is
So every thing she says ends up eloquent
She better be better
Than me

If I'd never met you I'd be happy now
I wish that when you walked towards me
I would've turned around

Kaya May

My mom just shook her head when she heard the news
That you didn't want me like I want you
She said "he's just not the one" - said it wasn't my fault
But I don't agree at all

Someone else might buy me things and meet my family
Take me places and try to make me happy
And I'll get drunk and try to feel in love
Let him kiss my lips like you used to
But I wanted it to be you

I know someday someone will love me back
I don't know much but I know that
God's got better plans for me than I do
But I wanted it to be you

He'll propose and I'll be fine
I won't be his but he'll be mine
He'll accuse me of still loving you
And I'll say I don't when I do-
Cause I
Wanted it to be you

Thought we were on the same page
But then you turned it on me
Thought you'd take off the pressure
But you just put it on me
You were supposed to make these days
The best ones I would live
But all you ever do is take
And all I do is give

I want to talk to you all the time
But I know that I can't
When you sleep halfway across the world
And I don't know where we stand

I guess I just
Loved too much
Said I miss you much too much
Fell much too quickly into love
I just had so much to say
Too much love to give away
I guess I just
Loved too much
And you did not
Love enough

You're like cold coffee

You're still sweet but I don't want you anymore

You're the crumbs that fell onto my jeans

And then off to the floor

You're like the food that went cold on my plate

You cost me something but

Now it's too late

You're the bustle of voices all trying

To outspeak one another

You're the couple in the corner and

The daughter and her mother

She has polka-dotted bows

Tied around her hair

And I swear you are everywhere

It's strange because I always knew
I was too good for you
Not in the way I look but in the way I am
For you I moved a hundred mountains
And you didn't lift a hand

Kaya May

Every thing that you did
Only ever led me on
Led me down a path that I
Wished that I lived on

You moved on so quickly
I barely saw you leave
It's hard to remember who
I was when you loved me

Oh my love, now I see
Why you're still single at your age
When commitment stands in front of you
All you see's a cage

I don't want a part of your heart
If she still lives in it
For I know I cannot fit
Into the space she left
When she moved to California
She left her baggage in your chest

Kaya May

It's so interesting to me
That I'm no longer what you need
And still you refuse to leave
Why won't you end it before I do
You're the only one in this room
Who is still in love with you

I sincerely hope that you
Are doing better than me
But I hope someday you start to wish
I was singing in your front seat

Kaya May

I remember a boy who used to take pictures of Kayak signs
And say they made him miss me
Could've loved me forever but decided to list me
I remember a boy who said that he'd give me his last name
And instead gave me away
Promised me he wouldn't leave
And moved to another state
I remember a boy who said he loved me
And for the first time I said it back
I remember a boy who was a train
When I was just a track

You said we'd go to dinner
Said you'd play with my hair
Said you'd show me off
Take me anywhere
You said you hoped after this trip
"Like" would turn to something else
But love you are a narcissist
You only love yourself.

Kaya May

The spotlight found you so you ditched me
Didn't meet your star quality
But I liked you before you were cool
I guess that makes me a hipster
And that makes you a fool

The last night you spent with me
You didn't touch me once
For you were far too busy
Falling out of love

Kaya May

That little blue arrow that points to the right
Stupid how much it signifies
You never called me on the phone
Just sent me DMs
Now we don't even talk
We're not even friends
You went from treating me like nobody had
Shaking the hands of my Mom and Dad
Taking my time and leaving your shirt
Not wanting enough to make this work
From slow dancing in your boots in your driveway
To having nothing
Left to say

I fell in love with you from the backseat of your car
Watching your eyes in the rearview mirror
You can keep your heart there in her chest
And I'll leave mine right here

Kaya May

You said your friends back home call me Chicago
And "the one that got away"
But I'm right here in your passenger's seat
You're the one that didn't stay
You said I'm trouble because tomorrow I'll leave
Just like I "always do"
But I'm right here in your passenger's seat
Screaming I never stopped loving you

There's an envelope in the fireplace
Half burnt but I still see your face
In the frontseat of my mind
Can still make out your name the same
On the return-to line
But I know if I pull us from the flames
I'll regret it in due time

Kaya May

I go to say I miss you
But it comes out in different words
"I'm happy you're happy
Even if it's with her"

It's been seven years and sixteen hours of living 700 miles apart
But in each state and on each date you still had my heart
Don't act like I didn't try
To find love in someone else
Don't act like I didn't try
To compromise myself
I tried for 2,555 days and you're still all I need
I hate how much I love the boy
Who never needed me

Kaya May

I'm going to go to Cinque Terre
The place where you proved to me
That I was foolish for believing
That you could love anything
You couldn't have me in that moment
So you retreated back to her
Shame on you for pretending that you were
Someone I could end up with, someone I could have
For you are just a liar- the best thing I never had

I'd gotten over you, you know? It isn't fair that you can go thirty days and nights without thinking of me once and then just hit me up because you saw I was doing well. I've been well, yes. On my own. You left me, you see. You don't get to have any part in the celebration of my successes because you withdrew yourself from my life. You can't waltz back in when it feels more convenient for you and your too-blue eyes. I'd stopped thinking about you at night. I'd stopped hoping you'd be mine.

How incredibly
Foolish of me
To fall for a tin man
To think that he could love me
When we all know he can't

I told you I missed you
But I should've kept it to myself
I'm realizing now you don't want someone
Unless they want someone else

Kaya May

We couldn't be more different
But couldn't be more the same
I would've given anything
If you'd given me your name

I hope one day you find you crave
The sound of my voice
I gave you time I gave you space
And you gave me no choice

Kaya May

You said I'm too much for you right now
And I said I'm just what you need
I think in time you'll realize
What was good for you was me

I want to say I miss you
But I know that I don't
I know I only miss
Not being alone

Kaya May

I've been deleting voicemails
And dyeing my hair
I'm not who I was
When I was there
In your room
And in your car
In your head
And in your heart
For you cast the next scene
And didn't give me a part

You're three feet in front of me
But you could've just as well not come
When someone gets too close to you,
You put on your shoes and run

Kaya May

I read other people's words
About how there is more to life than you
How there's so much to look forward to
How there are oceans to see and karaoke to sing
And leaves to watch change in the fall
But all I can think is if I don't get you
I don't want anything at all

I'm going to spend the rest of my life
Making sure you regret walking out of mine
I can't wait for you to frown at your words
Realize that you're disappointed with her
I know I'll find someone else
I hope you
Find yourself

You're permanently happy because you don't notice
How other people feel
The world you live in is fabricated but I can't
Prove to you what's real
It was endearing at first- the positive demeanor
Until I realized you tried love before
And realized you didn't need her

You don't like girls with brown hair
Maybe that's why I dyed it
I knew you wouldn't like it
So I had to try it
My will is weak
But my soul is strong
If you think I'm ruined
You are wrong
My hair got dark,
But my heart got light
When I lost you
I found my might

Kaya May

I loved you like a song and
You used me like the radio
In your stupid Ford
Hit play, pause, repeat on me
Whenever you got bored

My own body should not
Remind me of someone else
But I can't stop thinking of them
As hands that you held

Empty
That's what you made me

Bought me a gin and tonic and told me I was fancy

Empty
That's what you made me

Put your hand on my leg when you told me that you can't sing

Empty
That's what you made me

Played my guitar half-assed and only asked me to do one song
Stood in the spotlight and convinced me I liked to stand in the dark
Kissed me goodbye and I said to text me when you got home

Empty
That's how you left me

Alone

While I was getting hopeful,
You were getting hammered
For you I dropped my plans,
My dreams,
And my standards

Kaya May

It seems you forgot
How to pick up the phone
And I just got better
At being alone

I think the saddest moment I've experienced in quite some
time was when I read your three words that used to light up
everything they reached and I responded with three of my own:
"No
You
Don't"

Kaya May

You remind me so much of him
That I almost called you his name
Your faces have their differences
But your spirits are the same
I didn't know I missed him
Till I met you today

I know that this will hurt your feelings
Because you'll know it's about you
But I promise that was never what
I intended to do

Kaya May

I hope one day you call and I'm not there and my husband asks
if you want to leave a message - you pause, answer a little breathless-
"Yes I want to say I never should have worn her heart like a necklace"

I guess I'll start getting used to
How it feels to lose you
No more seeing your name
Light up on my screen
I know you're not
Coming back to me

Kaya May

It's funny how my mind works
I've begun to blend who he is
In with who you were
The way he liked me too much
Compensating for the way
You didn't like me enough
Your matching haircuts and uniforms
And blue eyes and big strong hands
Two boys my mind confused
And turned into a man

I wish his name wasn't in that book
It still stings every time it comes from a pastor's lips
Every time I have to consider acquiring
A last name that isn't his

Kaya May

He had a black cross tattoo
And his eyes were blue
And I miss him all the time
I text him every couple months or so
Though I know he won't reply
I turned him on and turned him off
Within 24 short hours
And I've spent the past six months on memories
I keep wishing still were ours

I didn't know it then
But you strung me along
You were a boy I could've loved
And now you are a song

Kaya May

We talked about God and evolution and the reasons that I left
Somehow ending up with our heads on my pillows and my
Hand in yours on your chest
I didn't like it when you talked about how you're
Seeing other girls
But it didn't bother me enough for me to say it hurts
When you looked at me and said I'd find someone and that I
Shouldn't give up hope
That didn't feel good to me,
I just want you to know
Because laying there I wouldn't have minded if you just leaned
In and kissed me
I still don't think we're for each other but I still want to know
You've missed me
Often I wonder if we're wasting days with other people
When we should eventually just come back
To what you knew already worked
When I didn't know that

I'm trying to wash you off my skin
But how do you kick out who you let in
The combination has changed since
The last time you tried to get in
Your code won't work like it did before
That key doesn't fit into my door
You may be what I was living for
But I don't live there anymore

Kaya May

Your flower finally died today
February March April May June
Five months of getting over you
But this time it was a different kind
Of end goal for the journey
This time I wanted to stop confusing
Love with how you loved me

He looked at me the first night we met and said
"Can we just establish that you're beautiful?"
And I wished he was you
He jokingly proposed when it was too soon
And I wished he was you
He asked to see me the day after we'd spent all day together
And I wished he was you
He introduced me to his sister and held my hand in church
And I wished he was you
He came up with activities, took me on dates without me asking
And I wished he was you
He took me to a party and introduced me to everyone he knew
And I wished he was you
He is the first person to treat me like I've always wanted someone to
And if I let him he'll ask me to marry him soon
Because when you love someone, that's just what you do
And I wish he was you

Kaya May

I think I'll take a roadtrip,
On a solstice,
Down a one-lane tree-lined street
To a town I went without
Where you never went with me
Get more okay with myself
And the reasons that you're gone
Let my wounds turn into scars,
Not listen to our song
Start putting new words in my head
And just me into my bed
You take all the time you need
I'll use it to remember me

If anything you taught me how
To get over him
Led me so far from his heart
That I stopped trying to get in

Kaya May

I think about you from time to time
And wonder how you are
Wonder if you tell every girl
About all your stupid scars
But who knows if you're
Even spending this time
Seeing someone else
All I've ever seen you love
Is baseball and yourself

"Why do you do it?"
They push a microphone to my lips and ask
I look down at my empty hands
And let out a little laugh
"When I stopped trying to keep hold of him
I finally had room for what wanted in
My motivation now is to become someone
He wishes he had held onto
Someone he wishes wasn't standing here
Saying this to you
And when this happens he will come back
Asking for another try
'But silly boy I am finally complete,
And thank you-
You are why.'"

Kaya May

To every boy who took
A piece out of my heart
You didn't make me stronger
But you surely made me smart

Looking For A Unicorn

I see versions of you everywhere
The you I hope exists
I've been thinking about and looking for you
Since I was a kid
I thought you had blonde hair and blue eyes
And a gap between your teeth
But he took his promise of forever
And moved to Tennessee
I thought you were a basketball player
Who introduced me to my favorite band
But told me that he'd met someone
"I hope you understand"
I thought you were a boy I met online
Who to me felt like home
But in a room with Jesus
He still felt alone
I thought you were in the Air Force
First when I was 17, then 23
But the first one left me hanging,
And the second set me free
I've thought you were a dozen men
But of one thing I'm convinced
Loving you will help me forget
That I once thought I loved him

Kaya May

Go with your whole soul into this world
And let it break you apart
For each time you're put back together
You're a whole new work of art

Looking For A Unicorn

At this point if I'm ending up with anyone
They're going to have to walk right up
To me and say hello
I'm so over searching that my eyes
Might as well be closed
May this be the year that I stop looking
For it's never done me any good
Since no one else decided to,
I'll treat me like I should
But I did find one thing
While looking for someone else
While looking for a unicorn-
I realized I had one within myself.